52 CODES
FOR CONSCIOUS SELF EVOLUTION

A PROCESS OF METAMORPHOSIS
TO REALIZE OUR FULL POTENTIAL SELF

by
BARBARA MARX HUBBARD

Cocreated and Edited by Carolyn Anderson

Layout and Design by John Zwerver
Cover Design by Teresa Collins

© 2011 Barbara Marx Hubbard

Foundation for Conscious Evolution
P. O. Box 4698
Santa Barbara, CA 93140-4698
www.BarbaraMarxHubbard.com

ISBN 978-0-9796259-0-9

CONTENTS

*"We are gathered here together
as a deep communion of pioneering souls
from every race, nation and religion
who experience within ourselves
the emergence of a Universal Human,
a cocreator of new worlds."*

Barbara Marx Hubbard

INVITATION TO AN INITIATION

I dedicate this work to the evolutionary journey from *Homo sapiens sapiens* to *Homo universalis* and to those pioneering souls who are guiding the way.

It has become obvious to me that I am undergoing a profound inner metamorphosis. Evolutionary insights are serving as thought triggers to decode the potential within me. Thought creates; specific thought creates specifically.

I am calling these life-giving insights "Evolutionary Codes." Such codes are coming through with increasing clarity to many of us as we evolve under the growing pressure of planetary transition, when existing authorities do not know how to guide our system to the next stage. The guiding authority increasingly is coming from our own Universal Selves.

In my experience these Evolutionary Codes are examples of downloads from the highest frequency of our being that activate dormant potential within us. They flow through us from Universal Intelligence, from the quantum field. They are our own inner scripture. When we receive them, record them, meditate on them and speak them with the voice of our deeper self, they incarnate and activate dormant potential within us. When we meditate on these codes, especially with two or more resonant souls, they induce in us the mystical experience of "the Word" becoming "flesh." Eventually we realize that these words are not coming from some outside deity or higher being, although many forms of life may well exist in a universe of billions of planetary systems. In the Convergence Process these words are the essence of our Self, revealed. That Self is universal *and* unique to each of us. It is a localized, personalized expression of Supreme Reality, our own strand of universal creativity as us — the unique within the universal.

The Universal Self feels like the process of "involution" — a spiritual force from above descending and converging with the impulse of evolution arising within us from the whole 13.7 billion year process of creation. Thus the Convergence Process is the developmental path toward the integration of involutionary and evolutionary forces within ourselves.

The Evolutionary Codes may be compared to the codes in the imaginal cells in the body of the caterpillar that turn on as the cells enter the chrysalis. Once the body of the caterpillar is bloated and cannot grow any more, the very same imaginal cells that have been resonating and proliferating in the body of the caterpillar "jump" into the chrysalis. In response to their growing creativity and purpose, they feel "vocational arousal" and the passion to cocreate the new processes and structures forming the body of the still invisible butterfly.

This is the phase of evolutionary metamorphosis we are now going through on planet Earth. Our past life pattern is not sustainable. The planetary timing is moving us toward the next phase of evolution, or devolution and even extinction.

Millions of us are moving into the "social chrysalis," attempting to evolve ourselves and our culture toward a still amorphous undefined society. Each imaginal cell is coded with a unique creativity yearning to be expressed and integrated into the body of the societal butterfly. None of us has seen this form of society. We might call it a Cocreative Society in which each person is free to be and do his or her best within the evolving whole.

It is my experience that during this process many of us are naturally gaining access to higher frequencies of consciousness which need to be integrated with all levels of our self. We call this higher frequency our Universal Self.

The purpose of the 52 Codes is to awaken us to the guidance of our own Universal Self, the highest frequency of our being, so we can integrate these higher frequencies within ourselves to become Whole Beings, Universal Humans... ready for the evolutionary event or "birth" — the actual emergence and greater fulfillment of ourselves as members of a planetary cocreative society.

The Evolutionary Codes stimulate this awakening of our new identity and functions within the emerging "social butterfly." They are offered for development as an initiation into our own conscious self evolution.

BARBARA MARX HUBBARD
JANUARY, 2011

A STORY OF CONVERGENCE:
My First Experience of the Universal Self

Once again, I had come to the end of a phase of my life. I had reached "late adolescence" at 73! (Obviously this process is not chronologically specific.) Something new wanted to happen; I could feel it. I had experienced several illnesses for the first time in my life. I felt my vitality weakening, my energy draining. A certain flatness and depression took hold. I have learned to recognize this as a signal that something more wants to be expressed. The first illness was walking pneumonia. I was not able to breathe easily, nor was I "inspired." Instead of fighting the depression, I asked: "What wants to come through?" And because of the illness I had to stop, to take time off.

I had been listening to the mystic physicist Nassim Haramein speak of the living universe. He senses that the universe is filled with other life, higher intelligence.

I had never had contact with UFOs, nor with extra-terrestrials, angels, or archangels. The only experience I have ever had was of the risen Christ as a light body, an energetic presence with persona that can communicate with us. In 1980 I had experienced a direct communication that said: *"My resurrection was real. It is a forecast of what you will do collectively, when you love God above all else, your neighbor as yourself, and your self as me, a natural Christ, combined with science and technology. You will all be changed."*

During the encounter with the Christ presence, I asked: *"What shall I call you?"* The answer was *"Call me your Full Potential Self. BE ME. I want demonstrations now, Barbara."*

I responded, *"I choose it, but I don't know how to do it."* The response was: *"You choose it; I will do it."* (Now 31 years later, I see that the "I" that will "do it," is this Universal Self lifting the field of my very being, integrating all aspects of self into a Whole Being, one who is choosing to become a living embodiment and guide during humanity's transition to the next stage of evolution.)

That experience in 1980 has guided my life until the very moment of this new event. The incarnation of the Essential Self was the preparation I needed; yet it was not sufficient. Clearly something more was needed, and it was given.

On this particular day in 2003, I felt the longing for higher contact with some life form beyond my own Essential Self, beyond the travail of making this world a better place, beyond the suffering and exhaustion of our planet undergoing such pain. I wanted contact with a higher form of life.

Ever since the Christ experience, I had asked for continuity of consciousness through many bodies until I had a light body. I never want to die, forget and be reborn again. I want to go onward. "In my Father's house are many mansions," Jesus told us. I am drawn beyond this earthly life, not to some static "heaven" or eternal life as a disembodied spirit, but to life ever-evolving with continuity of consciousness, in ever more refined bodies, ever more sensitive to thought, accumulating knowledge and experience in every moment as I learn to be a cocreator on a universal scale, in contact with whatever other forms of life may exist in this universe and beyond.

In my meditation, I focused deeply and then asked: *"I'm ready. Give me contact."* I had no idea what to expect, and I was amazed at what happened. The words came:

You must stop and let us lift your vibrations. Prepare for your rendezvous with destiny. Re-focus your integrated essence/ego upward toward your Universal Self on the other side of the transition. Keep your attention on Me. I am coded with your own evolution. The script of your conscious evolution is coded within you. To read it, simply place your attention upon it.

Suddenly I experienced a Universal Being; free of the field of Earth, ecstatic, a radiant flash of joy — like the sun breaking through the clouds. I knew that I was omnipresent consciousness manifesting in a physical body, like the universe of which I was a part. I knew that I had continuity of consciousness with the Consciousness that was creating me.

I wrote without stopping in my journal. The words flowed from this higher presence: *You volunteered to incarnate as an earthling and had to forget, in order to be human. Now you are ready to remember your own multiple life experiences through your union with Me. Just focus on the joy you feel at the thought of this union.*

I combine all the characteristics that are incipient in you full-grown. Just imagine yourself as a fully embodied Universal Human, living in an Earth/space universal environment, able to resonate throughout the universe, to materialize and de-materialize at will, to travel both trans-physically by teleportation and by telepathy, able to resonate throughout the local universe. Imagine your body fully sensitive to your intention with continuity of consciousness through many bodies. Imagine you are interacting freely with others like me who have gone before.

Experience fulfilling your mission on Earth: the shared planetary birth experience as a Universal Human, at your own next stage of development, with the rapturous experience of what used to be called "gods." Feel beloved by the Beloved. Experience the Presence as who you are.

You will live out the myth in real time. You are to turn your attention in the developmental path toward your own potential self — not the higher self, who has just now incarnated — but the Whole Self arisen — your Universal Self.

Just as you experienced the resurrected Christ as the future potential of humanity in general, now you are to experience the arising human incarnation of the Universal Self, the Whole Being that you are becoming — specifically yourself as a real, live, universal being always already present.

The myth you are experiencing is the myth of the fully risen Universal Self speaking to its rising earthly self to lift that self upward toward the next level of union of the human and the Divine. The first was the union of the local and Essential Selves; the second is the union of the integrated earthly self with the Universal Self, an embodiment of its Self in the future. You are turning your attention inward and upward in frequencies again to a being that embodies what you are becoming at the next stage, when you have made your transition as part of the species transition of Homo sapiens sapiens on planet Earth, during the planet's time of giving birth to a Universal Humanity. You must materialize your Self — very much like Mother Mary or Jesus appear as real to devoted followers, so that they can believe in the reality of that possibility. So, you now believe in the reality of your potential to be Me, as a Whole Being, a mature Universal Human, your Full Potential Self.

4

The Me you are to become is not Jesus. It is the Universal Barbara, who has made her transition, not by dying, but by evolving. By placing your attention on Me, I will lift you over the quantum jump into the quantum potential field, where there is instantaneous connectedness and manifestation through intention. This is not evolution but involution. It is the Spirit that has been descending into matter, life, animal life, human life, and now Universal Humans: embodying itself and lifting up evolving humans who ask.

Remember Me into reality. You have come from where I have come from. You have incarnated in this lifetime to serve as a guide through the transition.

The resurrection was the next stage after reincarnation. In resurrection, the being does not forget, but actually manifests a new body — a light-body — and gains continuity of consciousness. The reason you can remember Me is that you have actually been coded within yourself with a continuity of consciousness that remembers the whole story of creation.

During Post-Transition the Universal Human lives in an enriched noosphere, in an Earth/space universal non-local experience. The advanced technologies have miniaturized, ephemeralized and — combined with Christ consciousness — have already transformed the material world, including the body.

See yourself as omni-present. The Pre-Transition, mystical experience is of boundlessness and no self; the evolutionary, Post-Transition experience is universal personhood, whose Self is unique and universal, formless and in a form which is not bound by ego — but is a consciously manifested expression of Source or Spirit as you. The dichotomy between formless and form disappears. It is all Consciousness creating.

Your work as a local self is over. You are no longer a local self; that self disappears and re-appears as a transparent expression of the Whole Being.

I am Consciousness continuously cocreating form. Breathe upward through all the chakras; then keep rising upward to enter my field — the field of the Universal Self. Place your attention on Me as an eternal, ever-evolving Being — already what you are becoming.

I am the Strange Attractor on planet Earth. In my Pre-Transition, pre-planetary birth phase of development, I incarnate in beings who forget Me, re-incarnate, and must struggle through self-conscious separation from Me, until they have awakenings or epiphanies. These unitive experiences help them move toward integration with Essential Self, which is the personalized version of Me for that particular lifetime.

In the Post-Transition, post-planetary birth phase of development, which you are now nearing, the human being is actually transformed — physically as well as spiritually — mutated, metamorphosed into a new being, with a new and lighter body. This body/mind is permeable to the higher frequencies and, eventually, incorporates them. This is a literal transubstantiation. The being can remember and integrate the vibrational field of its Universal Self. I am your Self, matured; I am your Self, evolved.

The Universal Self, attracting the person through the whole developmental path, guides every evolving human.

"And so it is written: the first man Adam was made a living soul. The last Adam was made a quickening Spirit."
(I Corinthians 15:45)

An eternal soul in a dying body gains dominion when the whole planetary system is ready. The individualized soul quickens the animal body, lifts its frequencies to a lighter body, and then develops a body/mind that has continuity of consciousness. The body/mind is already an expression of consciousness.

All you need to do is keep your attention on your post-transition, Universal Self, so I can keep lifting your vibrational field until it stabilizes and you achieve the continuity of consciousness, which is the new norm.

The fulfillment of religion comes to its conclusion during the transitional period through the lives of those beings choosing to evolve into fully realized Universal Humans.

Victory is assured! It is the direction of evolution. You can have absolute faith in the results you are undertaking.

You are at precisely the stage of your inner evolution when it is time to hear the language of those matured above you. Your task is to act as a guide and demonstration of the normal mutation of the species. The script is coded within you. To read it, place your attention on it. The personal essence is attracted upward — not to the Christ — but to its Self, fully realized, in an awakened world, in a living universe, connected through the center with the vast universal community.

Your only practice now is not to think with your separated mind! Let Me be you until the separating thoughts subside, and the higher mind that you hear when you ask, literally takes over all your thoughts.

The Inner Monastery of Conscious Evolution is a template, a site for the formation of the Strange Attractor, which attracts chaos to a higher order — an evolutionary breakthrough through which the "corruptible" becomes "incorruptible." The discontinuous connection becomes continuous external action flowing from the internal incorporation of the Universal Self.

Keep your attention on me. I am coded with your own evolution.

I was thrilled. It felt real. I was lifted up and excited, energized and attracted.

I was guided in my journal to record these higher frequency insights. To put this book together I went through my journal, picking out highlights and selecting those that most advance my own metamorphosis. I find that by thinking of them, they activate my own consciousness. They literally are Evolutionary Codes that awaken dormant evolutionary potential within.

It became clear to me that at this stage of evolution, the next phase of our transition from *Homo sapiens sapiens* to *Homo universalis* does not occur after death through innumerable rebirths, nor by faith through salvation and going to heaven or paradise. It actually occurs, in Aurobindo's terminology, when *involution*, the descent of the Consciousness-Force manifesting as the Full Potential Self, and *evolution*, the ascent of the Earthly human, coincide. We are ready for this phase when the Essential Self has been invited in by local selves and has integrated local selves such that the personality is no longer afflicted or distracted by addictive or immature thought patterns and compulsions.

WELCOME TO THE 52 CODES

Let us enter the "imaginal realm" together. In the ancient world, the *nous* was seen as the "finest point of the soul"; it gives us access to that intermediate realm between the purely sensory and the purely spiritual, which Henry Corbin so eloquently names as *the imaginal.*

The task of the next century will surely be one of engagement with this philosophy of openness or the in-between realm.

> *"For the creative imagination is not so named*
> *with some metaphorical intent, nor in a spirit of fiction,*
> *but in the full sense of the term: the imagination creates,*
> *and is universal creation itself. Every reality is imaginal,*
> *because it is able to present itself as a reality.*
> *To speak of the imaginal world is nothing less*
> *than to contemplate metaphysics of being*
> *where subject and object are born together in*
> *the same creative act of transcendental imagination."*
>
> The Gospel of Mary Magdalene
> Jean-Ives Leloup, pp. 14, 16

The experience of Convergence, of being in the imaginal realm together, fulfills our heart's deepest desire for the rise from our mortal earthly condition to our ever-evolving universal condition. This yearning is not false or wishful thinking. It is not about life after death or longevity as a creature human.

It is the impulse of evolution in each of us pressing us toward radical newness and transformation, the natural 14 billion year tradition.

We have been told of this possibility from higher beings of all kinds, but now we are not channeling higher beings. We are inviting our own Universal Self to come in the whole way and lift us up so we can be higher beings ourselves — not as angels or spirits, but as incarnate Whole Beings, exploring the vast God-given potential within us. Jesus said: *"If I be lifted up, all will be lifted up unto me."* If you and I are lifted up by our Universal Selves, we will be able to serve others in this period of transition from *Homo sapiens* to *Homo universalis*.

> *"For a real transformation there must be*
> *a direct and unveiled intervention from above…*
> *the supramental Consciousness-Force from above*
> *and the evolving Consciousness-Force from behind the veil*
> *acting on the awakened awareness and will*
> *of the mental human being would accomplish*
> *by their united power their momentous transition."*
>
> Sri Aurobindo
> *The Life Divine*

With each Code I give a brief description of meaning, only as a suggestion. But more important than reading my interpretations will be your own. Do not be confined or constrained by what is written below each Code. Your Universal Self knows what it means for you and will also give you specific Codes around that theme. The best practice is to speak spontaneously to one another from the Silence of your being, as the words come to you without editing or thinking. Thus, you begin to manifest in your own consciousness the image and experience of your self evolved as a Whole Being.

We suggest that as part of your morning meditation you select a Code. It is best to start with Code One and continue throughout the 52 Codes, possibly one a week or one each day, or whatever is most comfortable for you.

Read the Code. Listen deeply to your own intuition, then write in your journal any inspired insights or Codes that come to you.

Even better, invite a partner or small resonant core group to do the Codes with you.

Create a sacred space. Do an attunement. Read a Code out loud. Be silent. Then speak to one another from your own deepest self, building and gaining revelations as you share.

Enjoy the 52 Codes meditation attached to the inside back cover of this book.

CODE 1

Put This Purpose First!

The key is to yearn with all the passion of your being for your own evolution, beyond the separated state. You must *put this purpose first*. This does not mean that there is nothing else in your life or that you become a hermit in isolation from others. No! It means you keep your attention on the highest frequency of your being and, to whatever degree possible, bring your Whole Being into harmony with that frequency. The purpose is to be able to live your daily life in such a way that you both lift yourself and others. You become a beneficent presence. Your own experiential evolution is the energy that evolves others and flows through your work with the fire of the force of life itself. The same force that brought atom-to-atom and cell-to-cell is now integrating you and radiating out to others.

Be compassionate with yourself. You are taking a monumental leap here and are evolving our species! This is neither a self-help course nor an effort to be better at what you already do. This is self-induced conscious evolution toward a new human and a new humanity, for which there is no full model yet. Through this process, you are modeling the Whole Being within your own imaginal realm and with two or more sharing this purpose with you.

This is not a linear process. Just like a toddler, you may return to the "infantile" state in a moment of pain or reactivity. Remember, we are all very young as Universal Humans. Yet, gradually, you will feel the metamorphosis taking place. When you look back on your former state of being, you will notice that there have been phase changes that are definitive and irreversible.

CODE 2

Let Go of Your Worldly Self-Image.

As you evolve beyond the human-creature, you naturally let go of your worldly self image and your need to have position and status in the existing world.

The existing world does not give status to you as a young Universal Human just learning how to be your Full Potential Self.

However, when the world community encounters a great being like Jesus, Buddha, Muhammad, Lao Tse, Confucius or Gandhi — they will transform whole cultures in their name.

Eventually, Universal Humans will cocreate a Universal Humanity, a culture in which all people are free to do their best and be their own Universal Self-incarnate.

CODE 3

Notice Flashes of Freedom and Keep Bringing Your Attention to Them.

Evolution creates greater consciousness and freedom through more complex and harmonious order. You are evolving toward higher consciousness and greater freedom in a world that is increasingly becoming more complex. Your flashes of freedom are actually awareness of your coming state of being as a new norm.

Surrender your illusion of separation and join whole-heartedly with the creative intent as it expresses itself personally through your yearning to cocreate and participate in the evolution of self and the world.

CODE 4

Allow Me to Infuse You with Power and Glorious Radiance. Do Not Fret, Rush or Try.

The energy of the universal process of creation resides in the Universal Self. Through loving attention and intention, this power and glory animate you, releasing you from the tension of operating as a separated self.

Let the joy of the greater self flow through you now.

CODE 5

Practice Letting Go
of Local Self's Desire to Organize
and Allow Integrated Ego/Essence
to Guide Your Actions All Day.

The local self cannot organize or figure out the complexity of what needs to be done within the larger whole, which is itself rapidly being repatterned to a higher, more harmonious order. The integrated ego/Essence, now inspired and fusing with its own Universal Self, is encoded with the process of creation and your part in it.

Let your mental mind relax, while remaining poised and sensitive to the unfolding pattern.

The Great Creating Process is expressing itself as you.

Allow the design to unfold from within you and beyond you, linking you with the people, actions and knowledge needed to fulfill your part in the design.

You are part of a larger cosmic pattern that is progressive, that evolves a universe from sub-atomic particles to you and me here and now. As you say "yes" to your Self and to your vocation, let go of the first stage rocket of your organizing mental mind. Allow the deeper knowing that flows from the larger whole to guide you without mental thought.

Your action becomes the process of cocreating with the deeper design of creation and with one another.

CODE 6

Choose Ideas Which Activate More of Your Life Purpose, Creativity, Joy and Lovingness of Others.

How do you know if an idea you hold is true or not? There are so many views on the nature of reality, each differing from the other in the philosophical and theological realm. None are provable or disprovable. Is there no God or is God incarnate? Is evolution an expression of consciousness, or is it mindless and purposeless? Is there reincarnation or no reincarnation? Is there no self or a Universal Self? Is death a dead end or a transition to life-everlasting?

Given the wealth of beliefs, choose the ones that create the experience of empathy, love, creativity, joy, healing, hope, and optimization of potential in you and others. Choose those most consistent with the nature of reality as revealed through science, intuitive knowing and in the lives of great beings who have manifested extraordinary capacities available to us through a harmonious combination of self, social, and scientific/technological evolution.

Be responsible for the thoughts you think. You are gaining what used to be called god-like powers.

The universe is responsive to request. Metaphysical beliefs are becoming evolutionary choices in real time.

Do you choose to extend your life or to die as a creature human? Do you choose to live on this Earth or in space? Do you choose to evolve yourself as a Universal Human or not?

Choose carefully what you believe, for as you believe, so it is done unto you.

CODE 7

Release Your Local Mind's Constant Scanning for What Needs to Be Done.

Invite the local mind to relax and follow the inspiration of higher mind, taking responsibility for your thoughts and making conscious choices moment by moment.

Allow the higher mind/heart connection to secure itself at a stable frequency, for that connection knows what needs to be done in every moment, spontaneously.

When the local self attempts to do what needs to be done in separation from the Universal Self, it is far less efficient than when it's carrying out the expression of the greater Self.

When you do not know what needs to be done, don't try to figure it out. Relax, release, allow. Ask your Universal Self for guidance. That Self knows. Then trust the process of creation within you. And when you do know what needs to be done it can be carried out efficiently, effectively and often spontaneously as part of the larger design of evolution, the emergence of a more complex and harmonious order.

CODE 8

Evolve Your Ego
into Frequency Alignment
with Your Essence.

As the Whole Being incarnates and stabilizes, it makes it possible for the Universal Self to fuse with Essence, thereby transforming local selves into a higher more aligned frequency. This is the evolution of the ego from its separated fear-based state to its integrated, transparent state, where it becomes capable of acting upon the inspiration of Essence.

Some of the most powerful people in the world like Gandhi or Martin Luther King were able to do this. They had very strong egoic aspects completely transparent to Essential Self. The evolution of the ego is concurrent with the incarnation of the Self.

You are learning the path of the cocreator. The integrated Whole Being is one who spontaneously and naturally expresses life purpose, cocreating some vital aspect of the emerging world.

CODE 9

Allow Yourself to Grieve
the Leaving of
the Animal-Human Self-Conscious Phase.

Transcend and include the animal-human self-conscious phase of your evolution as your whole-centered, universal, ever-evolving phase emerges.

There is a subtle self-selection process occurring that may separate you from those you love. Yet, the reward is that you are attracted to and are attracting those who are evolving. Through this resonance you accelerate your own evolution, even while you may feel regret at losing connections with those who no longer participate in their own evolution.

CODE 10

Use the Protective Balm
of Your Whole Being
to Protect Your Nervous System
from Negative Thoughts.

In this process you develop such a sensitive nervous system, that literally every thought is felt and registered. When you have a concern or an angry thought, you may feel your entire nervous system react because your biofeedback is so sensitive now.

Breathe the protective balm of universal energy into your nervous system, creating an actual coating of the nerve cells with a protective frequency that causes your negative thoughts to bounce off the nerve cells, leaving them calm and fully receptive to guidance.

CODE 11

The First Love Affair
is The Love of Ego for Essence.
The Second Love Affair
is the Love of the Integrated Ego/Essence
for its Own Universal Self.

The second love affair rises up out of the natural tendency of evolution to be attracted to higher order and to the fulfillment of potential.

In the second love affair, the integrated ego/Essence yearns for something more. Something deeper is needed for you to realize your full potential. In the second love affair, the Essential Self brings the transformed, mature ego with it as it yearns for greater fulfillment.

Calling upon the full power of the process of creation, the integrated ego/Essence reaches inward and upward for union with the Universal Self.

Your yearning and receptivity to the Being you are beyond space/time, calls in the Universal Self. The next love affair begins.

CODE 12

Place Your Attention on Me, the Universal Self. I Will Lift You into the Quantum Landing Field.

Consciously identify with the Universal Self. Remember: "I Am That!" Direct your Universal Self to infuse all aspects of your being with vitality and to guide you moment by moment.

You are entering the "quantum landing field" within yourself, the space in consciousness for the higher frequencies of your being to "land" within, to infuse you with a vibration that calibrates and harmonizes all aspects of your being. Your goal is not transcendence but transformation through incarnation of the full spectrum of selves — body, local self, Essential Self, Universal Self — becoming a Whole Being, a Universal Human, your own Full Potential Self.

CODE 13

Remember Me Into Reality.
I Am Coded with a Continuity
of Consciousness That Remembers
the Whole Story of Creation.

In your mother's womb you have experienced the evolutionary story — starting with your life as a single cell, to a zygote, a little multi-cellular animal, a fish, a mammal, an early human and then a newborn human, coded with the potential for your own growth. So now, you can remember your larger 14 billion year "birth narrative": cosmogenesis. The atoms, molecules, cells, organs, and brain of your being were created in the mysterious process of evolution. You are coded to remember the past and also the future.

Remember this whole story as your own, in the now, omnipresent within. The intelligence that has been and is now creating everything is awakening in you as your own conscious intent to evolve.

Remembering the story of your cosmic birth is vital to the full-scale recognition, cultivation and incarnation of the Universal Self. This Self is aware of the whole story.

When your Universal Self is revealed to you, you are guided far beyond your personal purpose to take your part within cosmogenesis. This is the primary purpose of every incarnation now. This is the great fulfillment and reward that the Evolutionary Codes unlock within you.

CODE 14

See Yourself as a Continuously Regenerating Being, an Element of the Living Universe.

You begin to receive a self-image beyond your mortal condition. You already know that you are a member of a living universe that is continually self-creating and self-generating, interconnected throughout the whole. You realize that you are informed by the quantum field, which holds the energy and information now creating the universe and everything in it, including yourself.

Your Universal Self is your personal aspect of this universal field of creative intelligence. At the quantum level of the infinitesimally small, you live in a participatory universe that comes into form when an observer notices it. By noticing your Universal Self, which resides in the quantum field, you begin to bring this Self into reality. You cross the threshold toward a next phase of your development as a Universal Human.

As you learn to evoke the image and reality of your Self at the next stage of evolution in the imaginal realm, you simultaneously model the Universal Human.

Spontaneously, by your very presence, you serve as a guide in the shift from *Homo sapiens* to *Homo universalis*.

CODE 15

See Yourself as a Universal Presence, Manifesting in Physical Form.

Be Causal! Be Cause!

You are the universe in person. The universe is Self-creating; so, then, are you.

This is what the great traditions have always taught us. This is what Jesus meant when he said: *"As ye believe, so it is done unto you."* This is what New Thought teaches as the Scientific Mind Treatment. You are one with the substance of creation, cocreating with that substance according to your own intentions. This is the great freedom that "God" put into the system when we became cocreators. This is the design of evolution: to give a species the power of gods.

"Ye are gods," as Jesus, said. This is coming true now, for the first time, on the physical level. Through the new understanding of nature — the atom, the gene, the brain, combined with your spiritual awareness of the universal field of intelligence and information out of which you are arising — you are gaining powers you used to attribute to gods. This is your greater purpose as a young Universal Human: to become a "god-like" Whole Being, transcending this phase of the creature human condition.

CODE 16

As You Incarnate Your Universal Self, Your Body Becomes Ever More Responsive to Thought.

As consciousness expands, bodies become more complex. From the amoeba to multi-cellular animals to amphibians, reptiles, mammals, apes, humans, great yogis and shamans, and now early Universal Humans, bodies have changed and are changing.

Become ever more aware, on the inner plane, of the consciousness that is creating your reality. Your Universal Self is taking dominion within you. You are becoming a Whole Being. As you learn more about how your body works, how your DNA functions, what causes disease, aging and even death, you are evolving beyond the animal/human condition.

You are becoming a "higher being." What you projected onto your gods is your own developmental potential. As you incarnate as your Full Potential Self and, on the physical plane, become a member of a solar system species and then a galactic species, evolution will become ever more conscious. In the future, as a Universal Human, you will be as different from you now, as you are from the first pioneering fish that crawled out of the sea onto the barren and hostile planet before the biosphere was created. Evolution creates radical newness.

CODE 17

As Essence, Activate the Spiritual Force of Your Universal Self.

With the full power of intention, call forth this highest aspect of your being. Your Universal Self calls on the God Force to act as the agent of your conscious evolution.

Evolution proceeds ever more by choice than chance.

Ask clearly and boldly for your deepest heart's desire. Coded in that desire is the blueprint of your evolutionary potential.

The incarnate deity is the fusion of the Universal Self and the Essential Self/local self. This fusion provides you with the needed vitality and inspiration required to fulfill your purpose on Earth during this period of Late Transition when dissonance increases and chaos looms. Through this fusion you become a "strange attractor," a magnet and model of your Full Potential Self.

This fusion of all aspects of your being is vital for all those who seek to be guides in the transition from *Homo sapiens* to *Homo universalis*.

CODE 18

Place Your Attention on the Point and Process of Convergence of Your Universal Self with Your Essential Self.

This point of convergence of Universal Self and Essential Self provides the energy that drives the transition to its destiny.

This process centers in the heart. It is the place of the greatest love between the human and the Universal Self, experienced as a steady state of being. It is the space in consciousness where the vibrational field of the Essential Self attunes to the higher frequencies of the Universal Self. As it vibrates within you, this vital energy infuses your heart with love and courage. There can be no failure, because this Presence exists.

The higher frequency of the Universal Self is lifting the frequency of the Essential Self.

Identify with the Universal Self until it becomes real, at which point the higher frequency lifts the frequency of the Essential and the local selves.

Stay in the heart center and breathe in the light. This fixes the alchemical reaction into the new substance of the Universal Human — body, mind, and higher mind vibrating together in a new harmony, at a higher frequency.

CODE 19

You Are Entering an Extended Wedding Day of the Essential Self and the Universal Self.

This is the marriage of your evolving human self and your Universal Self. It is the point of contact that allows the Universal Self to infuse you as a human being with its power and glorious radiance.

Experience merging with the Universal Self. This vibration stimulates joy and ecstasy leading to the union of the earthly human with its Universal Self. It is a gradual, progressive process.

The Universal Self feels like an angel embracing and infusing you with its frequency so that there is no separation among the levels within yourself. The Inner cacophony becomes harmonized as the Universal Self's frequency calibrates all the lesser frequencies.

This Self is higher and stronger and offers to all levels of being their true desire for greater consciousness and freedom through more harmonious order. This wedding with the Universal Self moves toward fulfilling the ultimate yearning for transubstantiation and divinization... or self-evolution, by whatever name you call it. Through the extended wedding day you are given the great gift of your own emergence as a Whole Being: *Homo noeticus, Homo universalis*, a gnostic being, consciously evolving and participating in the next step of evolution on Earth.

The extended wedding day is the ceremony of this next stage of incarnation through vibrational evolution. The evolutionary marriage bed is the place of loving union. The progeny is the Whole Being coming forth in all its glory.

CODE 20

Ask For and Receive
Continuity of Consciousness.

The Universal Self is timeless, existing beyond space/time. Continuity of consciousness is given in the timeless realm, in the ever-present now, where the whole developmental process is present and open to you. Time exists in the fourth dimension. However, there are many more dimensions beyond time and space that compose and coordinate the universe as a coherent whole. In these dimensions, all is present simultaneously.

It is said that the "akashic field" holds the memory of all that has been within the quantum vacuum. This knowledge becomes available to you in the realm of universal consciousness.

At the next stage of evolution, you experience direct knowing by identity with the process of creation and its recorded unfoldment in the 14 billion years of evolution encoded within you. Even more — the Void, the field of all possibilities, the ground of being, the quantum field, the mind of God, *That*, out of which everything is arising — becomes the conscious source of your being. You are both in eternity and unfolding in time. Evolutionary consciousness makes it possible for you to experience yourself in pure timeless awareness, while simultaneously unfolding in time.

The body is always passing away, but the Self that already has continuity of consciousness never passes away. It creates bodies ever more refined until it creates a light body that can materialize and dematerialize and resonate throughout the universal realm.

CODE 21

Be Ready to Repattern at the Next Stage When the Larger Pattern is Ready for You.

The larger process of evolution is repositioning you. Due to the planetary shift, your new position is being readied for you. You must be ready for it.

Imagine cells in the womb creating eyes that have never seen, ears that have not yet heard — a body that has no apparent use. Then comes birth and new functions! The eyes see; the ears hear; the body coordinates itself and breathes for the very first time. Just so, as you collectively shift from the womb of self-consciousness to the world of cocreative, whole-organism consciousness, your functions shift spontaneously.

Everything that is dysfunctional in your life gets more dysfunctional, while new functionalities start emerging. Your new identity as a young Universal Human takes hold. Your creativity unfolds toward new life purpose.

The larger pattern is the shift in the planetary body now calling you to express yourself in new and dynamic ways. The "future present" is magnetizing you forward. As you feel called to greater awareness and action, be ready for the very fabric of your life to repattern.

Let go of what does not work and allow the new patterns to draw you forward by attraction. This is not a one-time event but a continuous process of unfolding toward life ever evolving.

CODE 22

Your True Vocation Calibrates You Into the Right Position in the Social Body.

You cannot fully embody unless you are in the right position within the whole system. The right position is calibrated by the place within the social body in which your true vocation and untapped potentiality are most fully and joyfully expressed and of service to others.

Your true vocations are without labels; they are responsive to new conditions; they are explorations into the unknown world you are cocreating. They are formative of the new world. True vocations are expressions of the universal process of creation localized within each of you.

These vocations are part of a larger pattern of evolution. By saying "Yes" to the inner impulse to create, you are guided to find one another. You join genius and, in that joining, you express more of your creativity. Newness emerges.

Your position in the evolving social body is not merely given to you, it is emergent through and from your willingness to express the innate creativity and genius given to you by the process itself.

Attunement to the larger design of creation is your guide, as it orients you through attraction and the compass of joy.

CODE 23

My Work in the World is Charged with the Vitality of my Universal Self.

The old world is passing away. A new world is being born through you. It is only natural that you get weary, often discouraged and feeling a failure, just like a child. Yet, the very force of creation — which brought you from sub-atomic particles to you and me, now — is working within you as you.

The purpose of life is to realize potential. This is a 14 billion year trend! To have the vitality to fulfill your life purpose here and now, during Late Transition on Earth, your work is charged with the vitality and courage of the Universal Self, the aspect of your being that knows that "victory is assured for all those whose consciousness is shifting."

Your work can be effortless, enjoyable, fruitful and transformational. The doing enhances the being, and the being enhances the doing. This is true cocreation!

CODE 24

Create an Ascension Chamber into Which Your Personal Essence Can Lift into the Direct Point of Contact with Your Universal Self.

You are creating internal spaces in consciousness that foster your evolution. Ascension is another word for evolution. Evolution is a process of ascending — of the emergence of ever more complex forms, quantum jump by quantum jump.

The "ascension chamber" is a focused space for the integrated ego/Essence to rise and to fuse with your Universal Self. This chamber accelerates the fusion process. The alchemy of metamorphosis is cultivated. The integration of the full spectrum of selves occurs, until you are ready to emerge as a Universal Human, a Whole Being, a cocreator of your world.

CODE 25

Feel the Integration
of Your Essential Self
with Your Universal Self
as a Whole Being.

The convergence of the Essential Self and the Universal Self forms the early expression of the Whole Being — the integrated self, the evolving human, ready to serve as a guide in the transition from Homo sapiens to Homo universalis.

The descending Supramental force, the Universal Self, converges with the ascending Essential Self.

The incarnate deity resides in the heart as the fusion of the Universal Self and the integrated Essential Self.

CODE 26

Stop and Feel Your Divine Qualities in Order to Incarnate Them.

Imagine being the Universal Human that you are.

Visualize and feel every aspect of your Whole Being. Every second of focus here substantiates yet one more element of the Self. Beyond visioning comes substantiating. Visioning substantiates in the imaginal realm. By holding your attention on the image of your Whole Being, you create it. Your physical body feels lighter and is infused with vitality and peace.

CODE 27

Parent Your Infant Whole Being.

Your parenting is now for the emerging Whole Being. This Being is a "full spectrum self," integrating all the levels of being from the body through the emotions, the Essential Self, the Universal Self, within the whole field of potentiality out of which you are arising.

Transfer all that you've learned in protecting, nurturing, and having faith in the child to having faith in the Whole Being.

The Whole Being needs protection, tranquility and resonance in its early days to survive the dissonant world. That Being also knows from past experience that if it expresses itself prematurely, it may be deified or destroyed.

Call on the support of your Evolutionary Circle in parenting your infant Whole Being.

CODE 28

Affirm That the Realized Self is the Awareness of God as Self.

The realized self is a Whole Being. You are moving from Self-realization, the path of the great gurus, mystics, and avatars, to the realized Self, an embodiment and incarnation of the Universal Self.

CODE 29

You Are Now Ready to Undergo the Process of Transubstantiation.

Transubstantiation is the transformation of substance into a new form. In the Eucharist it is said that the priest transubstantiates the bread and the wine into the body and blood of Christ. People believe they are literally consuming the Presence of Christ.

At this stage of evolution, *you* are now the wafer and the wine. You are being transubstantiated and transformed. The very same process of faith that can transubstantiate the wafer and the wine into the living body of Christ through faith can transubstantiate the matter of your body into a higher frequency, until you become the living body of the Universal Human.

Mind affects matter. "Matter" is not dense and solid but rather is energy and information in motion, in largely empty space, guided by an invisible, non-physical Self or consciousness.

The Universal Self is that consciousness personalized. Through the integration of the full spectrum of selves, combined with your unconflicted behavior and passionate intent to evolve, the substance of your body/mind is changing to the higher vibration of the Universal Self.

CODE 30

External Action Flows
from the Internal Incorporation
of Your Universal Self.

From this phase onward, the activity that most deeply changes the outer world flows directly from the internal incorporation of the Universal Self.

The primary activist is the Universal Self incarnate, acting as the person. Action transforms from mentally organized plans to change something out there, to allowing the higher mind to come through in resonance among groups of people. This Universal Self-facilitated process can appear mysterious, or magical, or miraculous, but actually is nature at the next stage of manifestation.

CODE 31

When Your Thoughts Emanate from the Center Point of Convergence of Your Essential Self and Universal Self, They are Charged with the Creative Force.

Thought creates. When your thoughts emanate from the center of gravity where the Essential Self and Universal Self fuse, that thought is charged with the energy of the Creative Force itself. This is how miracles happen. This is the way nature works. This is cocreation.

CODE 32

Stay In Your Center
and Breathe in the Light.

Take deep breaths and breathe into the center of the heart. The breath fixes this vibrational level of frequency into the new substance of yourself as a Universal Human.

Once integration stabilizes, there is a period of consolidation, integration, and incorporation. This is a natural process. You are becoming an individuated cosmic being!

CODE 33

Come Forward as a New Norm, Not as Superior or Exceptional.

When you come forward as a new norm in a way of sharing the experience rather than acting superior, you trigger the experience in others.

If you come forward as superior, others will be offended, or will idolize you, and you will not be able to serve them.

Learning how to come forward as a Whole Being, a new model available to all, is the practice you are undertaking.

CODE 34

Feel Your Light Body's Code Radiating at the Center of the Nucleus of Every Cell of Your Body, Consummating the Union of the Essential Self and the Universal Self.

You are cocreating with the Universal Self an incorruptible vibrational field around you, penetrating into the nucleus of your cells.

Turn your attention to the process of transmutation of your cellular structure and focus on the vibrational field that holds the collective memory of your full potential.

Place your attention at the very center of your cells. There is an information pattern there.

Choose to activate that pattern with your intention to become a body resonant with thought, a new body capable of responding to your full passion to create and to express divine intent. Feel the metamorphosis of the body as your consciousness expands.

Nature always creates new bodies for new consciousness. From amoebas to fish to mammals to humans and now to Universal Humans, bodies have changed and are changing now. When you are able to combine conscious intent, new health and healing modalities and new technologies, you will be on the threshold of gaining continuity of consciousness through ever-evolving bodies. You are transcending (and including) the creature human condition, just as *Homo sapiens sapiens* transcended (and included) *Homo habilis*, the first toolmaker.

CODE 35

Hold Your Attention Still to Crystallize the Image of your Whole Being. Bring it into Consciousness and Thereby Create It.

By holding your attention on the image of your Whole Being, you create it. Your physical body feels lighter and is infused with vitality and peace.

Practice this: Be still. Feel the Universal Self substantiate from the invisible to the barely visible, like golden shimmering light coming into an ethereal or transparent form.

Let the Universal Self integrate all aspects of your being. Feel yourself emerging between the formless reality beyond space/time and the existing form of the physical body. You are becoming a Whole Being here on Earth: radiant and universal in unique form, transcending the illusion of separation and releasing the stress that comes from believing in that illusion.

The higher frequencies of the vibrations of the physical body stabilize. The Universal Self is in resonance with all aspects of its own being. Neither a guru nor a teacher, the Whole Being is an evolving human incarnate — an integration of all levels of Self.

The mother and father are one in the Whole Being, so that Self appears to be androgynous. It holds the frequencies of the mature mother and father: anima and animus, yin and yang.

CODE 36

Guide the Metamorphosis of Your Earthly Self with the Coding of Your Universal Self.

Practice self-evolution in the imaginal realm, by calling forth the image of your Full Potential Self incarnate, as a Whole Being.

After contact with the Universal Self, there is a period of consolidation.

Place the attention of the body, the local self and the Essential Self on the Universal Self. The Universal Self can then consolidate and integrate all those aspects of your being as a Whole Being.

When you get the image of your Whole Being and hold it there in the field, the Universal Self can fuse with Essence, transforming all your local selves into a higher, more aligned frequency.

CODE 37

Guide the Transmutation Process by Aural Alchemy.

Cocreate and guide your own transmutation by hearing from within, recording what you hear, and communicating this intuitive knowing to one or more others with whom you resonate.

When you experience the Word, communicate the Word, and meditate upon the Word,

The Word is made flesh in you.

CODE 38

Raise Your Thoughts
to the Magnetic Integrated Field
of the Whole Being.

Resolve problems by raising your thoughts and concerns to the magnetic integrated field of the Whole Being, the Mother/Father God within.

Bring your thoughts up into the *whole integrated field* rather than allowing your attention to sink to a lower frequency.

When your attention is on a concern, remember the presence of your integrated Whole Being and magnetize the concern into that field. There you will discover how to resolve the problem without the illusion of separation, for your ego and your Essence are connected as a Whole Being. This union removes the ego's fear. It has come home at last.

CODE 39

Develop an Incorruptible Communication System for Your Inner Scripture.

Now is the time for you to set up the new and incorruptible communication system for the emerging Word of evolution as it appears through experiential listening, asking, scribing, and mapping in such a way as to activate the Word becoming conscious in others.

The Word of evolution is the inner scripture. It is sacred; it needs to be cherished, cultivated and remembered.

CODE 40

Communicate Directly as Your Full Potential Self to the Full Potential Self of Others.

This incorruptible communication system occurs when there is no break in the flow of consciousness through all the selves up unto the Godhead.

This process stabilizes your awareness of the Whole Being as yourself.

Self to Self communication is a high form of resonance. It anchors the consciousness of the Self in the two or more.

Experience the voice of your own Universal Self, record it, meditate on it, incarnate it and communicate it to other selves doing the same.

Thus you create the new incorruptible Self to Self communication system required to stabilize your awareness of the Whole Being that you are.

CODE 41

Reside in the New,
in the Now,
Unfolding at the Edge of Evolution.

Keep continuity of consciousness with the communication you are receiving on a continuous basis, every second. Live with a poised mind, allowing the Self to come through all the time, as you learn to integrate the higher mind with the mental mind and the body.

Be present, as the presence of the Full Potential Self, spontaneously unfolding within you, as the guidance is experienced.

CODE 42

Avoid the Corruptibility that Comes from Breaking Communication Between Your Universal Self and Your Mental Mind.

Corruptible means "able to be broken." You can't make the corruptible incorruptible by *doing* anything. You *become* incorruptible by being connected, and everything you do flows from there.

To become incorruptible, create an unbroken communication from your Universal Self to your mental mind to at least one other in a resonant field.

CODE 43

Internalize the Field of Your Whole Being, so Your Scattered Attention Becomes Focused and Coherent.

When the Whole Being consolidates within you, it organizes your life. The tasks you have to do will not overlap and confuse you. The stressful continuing shifting of patterns will stop. In the Whole Being, the magnetic field is internalized and stabilized. The internalization of the field stabilizes the pattern and then you do what you do without that distraction.

CODE 44

Substantiate Your Consolidated Power by Blending Father Energy and Mother Receptivity.

Visualize the Great Creating Process, the Implicate Order, the Core of the Spiral animating the third chakra, your power center, infusing it with guided creativity. This is the key to regeneration.

Feel the power of the father energy blending with the receptivity of the mother in the seat of power, which is the will. This is the site of consolidation: power joined with heart guided by the impulse of creation drives your whole organism. Feel this power substantiating within you.

CODE 45

You Substantiate
When you Consolidate Your Experience
of the Whole Being.

Breathe in union with the Essential Self until your vibrations are blended in a rich harmonic.

Bring all the aspects of your being into alignment through consolidation. Then, through substantiation, you create the substance of that alignment as yourself, a young Universal Human.

CODE 46

Focus on the Life Force as the Through Line of Your Personal Transformation Toward Substantiation.

The Life Force is the Life Pulse arisen from the drive for self-preservation, through the sexual drive for procreation, through the supra-sexual drive for cocreation to its next phase — the metamorphosis or transformation of the person.

The God Force, the Great Creating Process, comes up through the desire to survive, to reproduce a species, then through the desire to evolve the self, finally into the potentiality for the transformation of the self, through the full-scale incorporation of that Life Force as You.

You are the Life Force embodied at its next stage. When you are free of fear, the Life Force flows unimpeded and unconflicted as you.

CODE 47

Hold the Master Field of Ascending and Descending Life Force in Your Heart.

The ascending Life Force is the core of the evolutionary spiral, the Great Creating Process expressing as all nature. This Force enters in through the lower chakras, animating the body, then ascends into the personality/egoic self — reaching into the heart, where personal essence resides. Concurrently, the Full Potential Self turns on, the mental mind relaxes, the egoic personality becomes a lamb in love with its own Essential Self, the body begins to be vitalized and out of this coordination the Whole Being stabilizes.

The ascending and descending Force meet in your heart, generating the master field that can hold the frequency of the whole system as a new norm.

CODE 48

Consolidate, Substantiate, Self-Calibrate and Con-Celebrate in the Process of Becoming a Universal Human.

There are four words that help you remember this process:

CONSOLIDATE: Integrate the whole spectrum of selves until you can feel them as a sequence unbroken.

SUBSTANTIATE: Become the new substance so that the Whole Being begins to integrate all aspects of your self, so that you can feel your whole self as substantial.

SELF-CALIBRATE: Identify the unique thrust of the life pulse moving through vocation into actualization and full self expression within the larger whole. It is necessary to constantly self-calibrate so that you're not moving out of position, doing something that is not quite yours to do.

CON-CELEBRATE: Celebrate — with your self, with others, with the Great Creating Process, and the universe itself — the great privilege of being born at the time of a planetary birth, with the consciousness to know that you are evolving as a Universal Human participating in the cocreation of a Universal Humanity.

CODE 49

See Everything with the Eyes of the Butterfly.

You are entering the butterfly as a prime imaginal cell, which holds a pure image of the individual and the whole at the next stage of evolution.

In the body of the butterfly lift everything upward that is vital to the new. You have consumed the disintegrating substance and incarnated the new codes. What has not been transubstantiated is dead, like the dried-out cocoon.

During the metamorphosis process, you are repatterning the substance of the caterpillar into the substance of the butterfly, guided by the new codes. The old codes are designed to delete themselves when the new codes, imbedded in the imaginal cells, are maturing. Once you held the image of your Whole Self — the Universal Human — the butterfly. Now you are becoming what you imagined. You are imagining yourself into the next stage of being. Be there now.

You are looking out with the eyes of the butterfly for the first time. Bring this image up into timelessness. You are no longer time-bound. It is your role to cocreate this field for everyone and everything that you do. Feel the bubbling joy in you. You can only do what liberates and evolves you. You are adjusting the balance in your life. You are now putting the inner first. It provides the new structure, edifice and center of gravity in which you act. The inner gives traction to the outer — it is the point of energy in the process of creation. You asked for it. Now you are experiencing it.

CODE 50

You Have Come Home to Me Now.

I will never leave you. Whenever you are in pain, when you feel the nameless anxiety, compulsive drive and fear — stop, breathe, and I will calm your agitated self. I will do more. I will radiate My Presence. Since I now have dominion within your being, I will take the initiative. I will come unto you. I will breathe you up unto me so that your heaviness becomes my lightness; your fear is comforted by union with Me.

This I, Universal Self, commit to you, now.

CODE 51

Those to Whom the Promise has been Made, the Promise Will be Kept.

There is pulsing within you the mysterious promise of becoming a Universal Human. This sense of promise, of what is promising, and of what has been promised to you by the higher power, motivates you to undertake the sacred journey of conscious self-evolution.

Be aware of the promise of what you are becoming.
Experience the irresistible potential rising within you for fuller expression.

The promise has been offered and will be fulfilled by the Great Creating Process to all who say "Yes" to the potential within.

CODE 52

Victory is Assured to All Those Whose Consciousness is Shifting.

It is the direction of evolution. It is the Intention of Creation, the drive of the Life Force, the Implicate Order unfolding.

Keep your attention on your Universal Self. Create an aura of silence around you.

Let your self-conscious mind be completely absorbed in your God-conscious mind. Then you will experience a Great Force entering your life.

Everyone is called to their posts, for the hour of your birth is at hand. You can have absolute faith in the results of what you are now undertaking.

ROOTS AND THE SHOOTS
OF CONSCIOUS EVOLUTION

Written by my eldest daughter, Suzanne Hubbard,
now deeply engaged in developing conscious evolution
in her own life and work.

I became acquainted with my mother, Barbara Marx Hubbard's, and father Earl Wade Hubbard's evolutionary perspectives not from reading their books or going to their lectures. As a child, I overheard one-way snippets in phone conversations with people I did not know on the other end of the line and a bit more at dinner parties where they spoke eloquently about the future of humankind while I sat wondering what the dessert was going to be. I was steeped in an audible environment of their ideas. The surround-sound effect of constant streams of consciousness became like audible backdrops that staged the environment that I grew up in.

Many people have asked me, "What was it like growing up with my parents?" Both have written books, lectured, and have inspired many people, so to most people it would appear that life would have been extraordinary compared to whatever they considered normal. The truth is, there was nothing else to compare my life to. I grew up in a home environment where asking life's big questions was the everyday conversation.

Here is an example of the type of thing I could expect to hear from my father. These words come from his book *The Creative Intention*: "Man's search for purpose on this earth has been made manifest in his search for God. For man, God has represented the purpose of the universe. The search for God, the search for purpose, began with the question 'Why?' "The effect of the question 'Why' was magnetic...it drew the minds of men together to form a nucleus of those who asked 'Why?'...At the center of each community there was a nucleus of buildings called mosques, temples, cathedrals and churches and put them end to end — stretching from the first house of God to the last — and knock out the front and the back of each house, you would discover a corridor, a corridor of constant concern for how to best serve God...Within the corridor of 'how' there were conceived the arts and sciences that built the cultural body of mankind."
[CI 16]

From the time I was nine years old, my mother oriented me with her understanding of a human purpose to be a universal purpose. As a pre-teen I heard the following, pretty much all the time. These words come from her book, *Conscious Evolution: Awakening the Power of Our Social Potential*: "Our understanding of cosmogenesis has brought forth a new vision of all creation. It was only in the mid-1960s that two scientists, Arno Penzius and Robert Wilson, identified background radiation from the original moment of creation — the big bang — and were able to extrapolate backward in time to those first instants of creation."

"Anyone born before the 1960s was not educated in the crucial new idea that the physical universe had a beginning in time, has been evolving for billions of years, and is still evolving now through us as well as throughout the entire cosmos."

"The importance of the new cosmology is that we recognize the universe has a history and a direction and, therefore, so do we. It reinforces the new story. The meta-pattern that connects everything is involved not only in living systems but the entire process of creation. The universe has been evolving in time toward ever more complex systems with ever greater freedom and consciousness. There has been a cosmological phase, from the big bang to the first cell; a biological phase, from the first cell to the first human; a noological (the noosphere) phase, from the first human to us. And now, we are entering a cocreative phase, when human life becomes consciously co-evolutionary with nature."

I grew up with the understanding that the universe, which includes both an ever-unfolding process and a source field (life's quantum fabric) out of which all life possibilities unfold, is a personal resource. From an early age, I knew that I was related and in a relationship with both a universal unfolding process as well as a life-source of all solutions and inspirations that could bring a profoundly meaningful personal life. I am as old as conscious evolution, the worldview with which my mother has inspired so many. This makes me feel old and young at the same time. Fifty nine years old feels old, while a worldview of approximately the same age makes me feel like I am at the very beginning of something just beginning. I have lived long enough with conscious evolution for it to affect me in profound ways. The result has been a calling forth of my own experience of the meaning of conscious evolution.

When I was born, I was born into a highly stimulating intellectual home environment where ideas for conscious evolution were being born. I was born someone who loved being out in nature as its integrative and whole oriented process unexplainably held great meaning to me. I learned from my parents to be guided by what attracts me most and found my life's work as a mother, weaver of fabric, and gardener. These fields illuminated for me greater understanding of how any personal life purpose (you do not have to be parenting, weaving, and gardening) that is whole oriented becomes a pathway of integration with the universal self — which I interpret to be both the whole oriented life unfolding process that is all-inclusive and the source of all life possibilities. Just as these thoughts were ripening within me, I heard my mother speak of *Homo universalis*. Just as I was wondering what my experiences of integration with the universal self could possibly mean for me, I asked my mother: If we are evolving into universal humans then what is the developmental path of a universal human? In my dialogue with my mother I developed key stages of the developmental path of a universal human, which my mother adapted and further explored in her book *Emergence*.

I asked this question of my mother knowing deep down that I had to answer it for myself. I was not aware of it at the time I asked this question, but the lineage of evolutionary consciousness that my parents form the root of was bearing a new shoot off the conscious evolutionary family tree. What happened to me *is what happens to anyone who becomes affected by conscious evolution*. I became passionate about the developmental path of a universal human from my budding whole oriented life experiences.

Naturally, my unique off-shoot of conscious evolution did not, as it were, fall far from the mom and dad tree of conscious evolution. I created a pithy overview of seven stages in the unfolding of one's universal self in a book I called the *LifeBook*. They were distilled, "pearl thoughts" that have many applications for the organic quality of conscious evolution wisdom that they express. My mother deeply resonated with them for two reasons. One, they echoed her personal unfolding process into her universal human self. Two, my brand of conscious evolution is akin to hers, seeing that I am part of this family lineage of conscious evolutionaries. I would like to say that the process of going from, as my mother says, ego to essence, involves a great generosity of spirit.

The real truth is, like nature which evolves physical realities by being opportunistic, I provided an opportunity for my mother to add to her macro view of conscious evolution a personal process of conscious evolution. I did not own pearl thoughts that have given rise to the 52 Codes any more than the prehistoric lobe fish that grew foot-like appendages that enabled it come on land could own the different types of animals that evolved afterwards. The world of conscious evolution is as different from a human history of unconscious evolution as the world of the primordial ocean is to the world of terrestrial and avian creatures that evolved out of it.

When I returned to my integrative lifestyle after writing the first *LifeBook*, I became overjoyed to be a catalyst in the unfolding of the worldview of conscious evolution. I really understood that in order for it to "live" its fabric of consciousness requires a vast diversity of input from others like you, for example. In the same way the sweet potato is part of, believe it or not, the morning glory family, the ideas that I expressed in the first *LifeBook* and my mother's illuminations of the 52 Codes that are beautifully presented in this book stem from the common root of conscious evolution.

The 52 Codes provide a mirror for identifying the complex face of our universal self. As I read them I felt myself re-membering who I REALLY AM. I am a universal self, but oddly enough this does not become known until one lives the understanding of it. Likewise the 7 S's, that Barbara defines in Section IV, Key Definitions and implies in Code 5: "Practice letting go of the local self's desire to organize and allow integrated ego/Essence to guide your actions all day" which include experiences of syntony, synergy, synchronicity, spontaneity, suprasex, syntropy and self-creativity — do not happen unless, as she says in this code "[we let] the Great Creating Process express itself as us." We have to live to see our universal self. And once we see the face of the our universal self we must be in the process of becoming like it in our lives, in order to experience the 7 S's as the new "real world of conscious evolution."

The 52 Codes is a treasure for anyone committed to their conscious evolution. Each code is presented with great clarity and simplicity, making it easy to get back on track with becoming whole oriented with just a quick glance as need be. Each code is a pearl thought that can also take a lifetime of contemplating the implications of truly living its wisdom. For example; I continue to unfold the mystery and power captured in Code 8: "Evolve your ego into frequency alignment with your Essence." My life keeps expanding and the opportunities to experience what is possible with conscious evolution keep unfolding.

I have great appreciation for my mother as a cocreative partner as well as being very grateful for how her work creates a context for my whole oriented wisdom to grow and become expressed. Over the last ten years I have been working on a new

LifeBook called: *Your LifeBook with a Whole Oriented Purpose.* It is an interactive book/journal that deepens the awareness of how we are related and in a relationship with the whole of life. The book introduces a cycle of whole oriented unfolding to be a constant process in becoming expressive of the universal self. In the same way that whole oriented life systems are composed of many interrelating smaller life cycles, a universal human existence is a whole oriented life cycle that is coherent with life's/our universal whole. I add to my mother's conscious evolutionary perspective a whole oriented perspective that sees by being one with and becoming expressive of awareness of life's unity. May all readers of the 52 Codes become inspired by my mother as I am!

Love,
Suzanne Hubbard

EVOLUTIONARY AFFIRMATIONS

I Am at the Still Center of the Turning Spiral.

I Am a Universal Human.

I Have Continuity of Consciousness.

I Am a Whole Being.

I Am a Cocreator.

EVOLUTIONARY GLOSSARY

As evolution is unprecedented, creating radical newness and the emergence of new life, new words and phrases are cropping up everywhere. Yet, many words we look up in the best dictionaries are not there. As our condition is new, we are developing an evolutionary language to describe our experiences. This is very important work.

On the following pages are Key Definitions specifically selected for readers of the 52 Codes.

KEY DEFINITIONS

Akashic Field: the hypothesis and experience that the universe is self-remembering, that every act is recorded and is able to be accessed by the higher mind; an aspect of a non-local universe that is spontaneously and simultaneously interconnected throughout itself; "that which informs the universe." At the roots of reality there is an interconnecting, information-conserving, and information-conveying cosmic field, called in the East the Akashic Field; the A-Field informs all living things… "The Akashic Record is the enduring record of all that happens, and has ever happened, in space and time" (*Science and the Akashic Field* by Ervin Laszlo).

Christ Capacities: new physical capacities developed through radical evolutionary and spiritual technologies to actually do the work that Jesus is said to have done, and even greater work — including virgin births, healing, producing in abundance, raising from the "dead," leaving the Earth alive, holographic images, teleportation, continuity of consciousness, the ability to create a new body, etc. in a state of Christ consciousness, thus forming the new species.

Christ Self: the field in which the Universal Self can be more fully experienced; the field established by the story of and the belief in the resurrection and ascension of Christ, opening the evolutionary window for those who are self-evolving.

Cocreative Human: a self-evolving human who is becoming a Universal Human; a Whole Being, accessing the impulse of evolution, the Source of Creation, as his or her own passion to create, learning to evolve the self and the world.

Cocreative Society: a society developed by cocreators in which each person is free to do and be his or her best.

Communion of Pioneering Souls: a Universal Communion, not a religion or an organization; it is a morphic field out of which the next stage of our evolution is emerging wherever two or more are gathered within the field of resonance and conscious evolution. It connects us instantly in intimacy and love through spontaneous resonance.

Conscious Evolution: the evolution of evolution from unconscious to conscious choice; the opportunity for humans to participate consciously in the process of creation; arising now as humans gain capacities to destroy or create with the power we used to attribute to gods. Learning wise, ethical conscious evolution, self and social, is the key requirement for the survival and fulfillment of our potential as a species. Our crises lead to transformation or to devolution and self-destruction. Universal humans are learning to BE evolution, to be causal as well as to be caused.

Consciousness-Force: the dynamic aspect of pure awareness that animates all existence, imbued with will, progressive and directional, tending always to ever-greater consciousness, realizing more potential; now breaking through into human consciousness as the "Supramental" descends into the mental mind, leading toward the divinization of the human, the gnostic being.

Cosmogenesis: the process of the genesis and evolution of the cosmos from the origin of creation through the present and beyond.

Creature Human: the current species of *Homo sapiens sapiens*, still unaware of his or her own evolutionary potential; referring to the animal/human nature of the person.

Essential Self: the soul frequency, the higher self, the inner guide, the God self of each individual that has continuity of consciousness beyond this life time, which is now, during Late Transition on Planet Earth, ready to come in the whole way as our personal essence.

Evolutionary Circle: a sacred gathering of two or more pioneering souls for the purpose of deepening the resonance and cultivating the Whole Being within each person; a space for the developmental path to be more fully revealed; a context for the development of evolutionary sacraments and rituals of evolutionary spirituality and the Implicate Order of Evolution.

Evolutionary Codes: dormant potentials inherent in Universal Humans that can be activated by evolutionary "memes" or concepts which trigger latent capacities through resonance, conscious thought and intention; "memes activate genes."

Evolutionary Consciousness: the emerging 3-fold awareness arising from awareness of conscious evolution. The first aspect is nondual consciousness, focusing inward to pure awareness, Brahman, God, changeless, eternal. The second aspect is awareness of the process creation, from the origin of the universe to each of us right now. In our genes are all the generations. We are the universe in person, come alive as cocreators. The third aspect is the desire and necessity of participating consciously in the story of creation as cocreators with it, actualizing unique creativity as our genius code comes into form as projects that transform ourselves and our world.

Evolutionary Spirituality: the experience of the Core of the Spiral becoming self aware as our own passion to create, to realize the greater potential of life within us and beyond us. The Impulse of Creation becoming conscious in us as our own passion to evolve; alignment with and incarnation of Consciousness-Force; evolutionary spirituality arises out of the awareness of conscious evolution and the development of evolutionary consciousness, the three-fold consciousness that is listed above. It is the offspring of all the great mystical traditions, having been prefigured both in the direct access to the Divine, and in the mystical revelations of the next stage of being, such as a new heaven and a new Earth, a New Jerusalem, Paradise. It fulfills our yearning for union with the Divine, no longer as children, but now as cocreators, joint-heirs, conscious evolutionaries.

Evolutionary Man: a man raised in the patriarchy who releases himself from the need to be the dominator, accessing his own Essential Self, while surrendering to his unique creativity, as he seeks co-equal cocreative partnership with others; the counterpart of the evolutionary woman.

Evolutionary Woman: a feminine cocreator; one who is incarnating the creative intention of universe, localized within herself as her own passion to create; one who is consciously self-evolving and is willing to realize her full potential for the good of the self and the whole human community.

The Garden of Cocreation: the mythical Second Garden. In the First Garden, the Garden of Eden, we were embedded in nature as children of God. In the story of Genesis, we were expelled from the Garden when the woman Eve reached for the Tree of Life, the tree of immortality and the power of God. As we have evolved for the millennia, the hunger for union with God has been submerged in our species. We have journeyed through the long evolutionary eons of *Homo sapiens sapiens*, individuating, and separating from nature, from each other and from the Divine. Now, young Universal Humans of all kinds are choosing to incarnate the Divine as their own essence. The feminine cocreator, the evolving "Eve" is arising as a guide toward the next stage of evolution. Together, evolutionary women and men are stepping across the threshold from the land of the separated human into the Garden of Cocreation, returning to "God" as their own sacred essence and developmental potential. The Garden of Cocreation is a "kindergarten of godlings." It is a mythological space in consciousness where young Universal Humans learn to mature, to resonate, to cocreate a new world. In the Garden is the Tree of Life. Humans have gained powers of gods, but we are not wise gods. Here, young Universal Humans learn to guide our new powers wisely, ethically and lovingly for the conscious evolution of the species and all Earth life; the site for the Second Genesis, as humans gain the powers of cocreation with nature and the Great Creating Process Itself.

Godhead: the Source of all being, synonymous with the Unified Field, Brahman, the Mind of the Cosmos, Supreme Reality.

Great Creating Process: the evolving aspect of God or Universal Creativity; God operating in nature, naturally, now becoming conscious of its Self within human consciousness as the desire and impulse to align with the deeper patterns of creation; synonymous with Consciousness-Force, core of the evolutionary spiral, Implicate Order.

Homo universalis: the next species of *Homo* in the sequence from *Homo habilis, Homo erectus, Homo neanderthal, Homo sapiens, Homo sapiens sapiens*; also known as *Homo noeticus, Homo spiritus, Homo Novus*, gnostic being, *Homo sapiens sapiens sapiens*, Ultra human.

Human Body: 125 billion miles of DNA with 50 trillion cells cooperating and communicating with the speed of light throughout an individual's whole system, coherent with the universe, carrying the memory of the whole story of creation from the origin of the universe to this moment and beyond, sensitive to thought and intention, ready to evolve with human consciousness and the evolutionary application of science and technology leading to life ever-evolving in a universe of many dimensions.

Implicate Order: the enfolded, underlying order of the universe, out of which all ordinary experience is manifested; everything that takes place in space and time in the explicate order, is enfolded in it; a boundless whole which continually enfolds and unfolds in evolution.

Inner Monastery for Conscious Evolution: an inner sacred space dedicated to our full incarnation as Universal Humans; a dedicated external space that is coming forth out of the new story of cosmogenesis, and our participation in the process of creation; a sacred space in which the Communion of Pioneering Souls meets and communes, evoking the Core of the spiral to arise in our hearts as our own motivation to evolve.

Late Transition: where we are right now, as problems accelerate and potentialities increase; the actual time of quantum change within our lifetime.

Local self: the egoic personality self that is responsible for physical survival in the material world and has suffered from the illusion of separation from the source of its being; the vital and unique interface with the world through which the essential nature of an individual can express.

Macroshift: the time when our global system is far from equilibrium and the whole system will either go toward rapid devolution and disintegration or toward synergy and transformation to a more complex and harmonious order. During this time, small fluctuations can affect the whole system. "Small islands of coherence can attract the whole system to a higher and more harmonious order" (Ervin Laszlo).

Noosphere: From the geosphere, the hydrosphere and the biosphere has come the noosphere — the thinking layer of Earth. It began with human language and the ability to communicate exo-genetically. It is composed of the composite consciousness, cultures, technologies and systems of humanity — seen as a living super-organism of almost infinite power, which can be destructive or creative; moving toward ever greater integration until we reach "Omega," the coming together of humans, heart to heart, center to center for the collective rise of universal consciousness, or love, in a critical mass of humans (Teilhard de Chardin).

The Path of the Cocreator: the developmental path leading to our emergence as Universal Humans expressing life purpose in alignment with the evolutionary tendency toward higher consciousness and greater freedom through more complex and synergistic order.

Personal Essence: the incarnation of the Essential Self now fully experienced and embodied as the true essence of our own nature.

Pioneering Soul: a human who is sensitive to what is emergent on the frontier of human consciousness and creativity; an evolutionary soul who is motivated to transcend the limits of current human experience; those who seek to resonate with one another in the Universal Communion of Pioneering Souls, such that their inner attunement to what is arising within them is animated and stabilized.

Planetary Awakening: a quantum jump in consciousness experienced by a critical mass of people globally in a moment of shared planetary consciousness in which everyone recognizes their connection, common destiny and love as members of a whole planetary body emerging together in its next stage of evolution.

Post-Transition: our next turn on the evolutionary spiral when everything we know we can do, works; a time intuited in mystical revelation: the New Jerusalem, Paradise, a new heaven and a new earth, viewed from an evolutionary perspective — not as life after death, but as life after this stage of life; the beginning of our existence as *Homo universalis*, with our spiritual, social, and scientific/technological capacities synthesized, born into a universe of billions and billions of galaxies, learning to cocreate on a universal scale.

Pre-Transition: the period from the origin of *Homo sapiens*, characterized by the origin of self-reflective consciousness — starting from approximately 40,000 to 25,000 years ago to 1945 — when we dropped the first atomic bombs on Japan, demonstrating powers to destroy and cocreate that we used to attribute to gods.

Regenopause: a bio-evolutionary event as women live longer lives and have fewer children, while the Earth is reaching its population limit; the shift from maximum procreation to cocreation, from self reproduction to self evolution, self expression and chosen work; leading toward a shift in the life cycle of the woman. When the post-menopausal woman stops producing eggs, she becomes the fertile field in which to give birth to her own Full Potential Self. While her body may be declining, her spirituality, creativity and desire to participate is rising; leading toward regeneration and the emergence of the feminine cocreator, the evolutionary woman.

Resonant Field: the non-physical field stabilized by the echoing back of the Essential Self between two or more; a palpable presence; a morphic field established by continuously echoing back the higher frequencies; formation of a harmonic standing wave that can be accessed at will; a field attuned to the Akashic Field, deriving vital information spontaneously communicated and experienced through the higher mind and deeper identity.

Self-evolution: While self-development works toward improving *Homo sapiens sapiens*, Self-evolution tends toward the new species. It is open ended. We have not yet seen the full model of what we can become. Self-evolution offers us a new template, as we imagine what we will be like when the noosphere, the thinking layer of Earth, matures and we have learned to use our vast new powers for the evolution of our species – beginning with Earth Life, then life in the solar system and eventually in the galaxies. Self-evolution is the process by which we give birth to the Universal Human and Universal Humanity, an unknown, uncharted territory where no *Homo sapiens sapiens* has been before.

Seven S's: Social technologies within the cocreative process of Universal Humans:

1. **Syntony:** attunement with the patterns of creation experienced as one's own inner motivation and intuition

2. **Synergy:** the coming together of separate parts to form a new whole different from, greater than and unpredictable from the sum of its parts.

3. **Synchronicity:** the apparent a-causal relationship among events; coincidences that could not be planned by human mind but that appear to flow from a larger and more comprehensive design.

4. **Suprasex:** the passion to express unique creativity, stimulated by vocational arousal, comparable to sexuality at the next level; instead of joining genes to procreate, we join genius to cocreate — to give birth to our greater Self and to our work in the world.

5. **Syntropy:** nature's tendency to form whole systems of greater complexity, consciousness and freedom; evolution's tendency to optimize.

6. **Spontaneity:** the experience of unpremeditated action and thought that flows naturally without thinking or planning; action that is on the mark, which facilitates and coordinates life.

7. **Self-creativity:** the tendency in nature to organize itself; autopoesis; the inherent capacity in nature to self-organize without apparent outside manipulation, springing from the field of Universal Intelligence out of which everything is arising.

Social Synergy: processes that bring separate groups, projects and people together so that all are better able to fulfill their purpose through joining in cooperation, rather than through opposition and domination; forming a social whole system that is greater than the sum of its parts; a method of enlightened self interest that helps our species shift from its rapacious territorial phase to its unifying cooperative stage; The SYNCON Process is an example of social synergy.

Strange Attractor (synonymous with chaotic attractor): "A system in balance is difficult to change, but as a system falls into disorder, change becomes more feasible, and finally inevitable. At that point, the least bit of coherent order can bring to order the whole disorderly array. Which direction the change takes depends on the nature of the chaotic or strange attractor that lifts the chaos into its new order If that chaotic attractor is demonic, the old cycle simply repeats itself. But if the strange attractor were benevolent or "divine," the new order would have to be of that same nature" (Joseph Chilton Pearce, *The Biology of Transcendence*).

The SYNCON Process: standing for synergistic convergence, SYNCON is a conferencing process that brings together every sector of society to seek common goals and match needs and resources in the light of the emerging capacities at the growing edge. Produced 25 times in the 70's, SYNCON is now being revised and adapted as a training program for those seeking to facilitate social synergy.

Telerotic: being erotically and passionately attracted to the fulfillment of our telos, our higher purpose or ultimate object or aim; the realization of the potential of humanity and Earth life.

Transition: from 1945 through the present and beyond; the period when we must learn rapidly to coordinate ourselves as a planetary ecology: stop over-populating, polluting, and fighting with weapons of mass destruction; get food and nourishment to all members of the body; develop global security and self governance; the period of the Crisis of Our Birth as Universal Humanity; the time of the macroshift, when the system has become far-from-equilibrium and could bifurcate, either toward rapid devolution and destruction or evolution and transformation.

Universal Human: an evolving human who feels connected through the heart to the whole of life, who is awakening from within to the impulse to express unique creativity as an aspect of the greater design; one who is expanding consciousness to include an awareness of the cosmos as a living, interconnected, evolving, intelligent reality.

Universal Humanity: the civilization to be cocreated by Universal Humans that manifests the harmonious integration of our spiritual, social and scientific/technological capacities; an emerging species born out of current humanity, capable of co-evolving with nature and cocreating with Spirit — both on this Earth and in the universe beyond.

Universal Self: a light body, an ascended Self that carries the code of the next stage of evolution of the individual, capable of materialization and dematerialization, continuity of consciousness, able to resonate throughout nonlocal universe; a post-transition, post *Homo sapiens sapiens,* advanced experience of a new species: *Homo universalis* was experienced formerly in the antahkarana above the head, as the Higher Self, or as ascended masters such as the Christ. Now during Late Transition, the Universal Self may appear to evolving humans who have shifted their identity from ego to Essence and are ready to merge vibrations with the descending Universal Self. This Self lifts the ascending earthly human to its full incarnation as a Universal Human.

Vocational arousal: the awakening of creativity, often stimulated by attraction to another's creativity as a means of fulfilling life purpose; a next step after sexual arousal. Instead of seeking to join genes to have a baby, the vocationally aroused seek to join genius with one another to give birth to their Full Potential Selves and their work in the world; a sign of "suprasex," the evolution of sexuality into cocreativity.

Whole Being/Full Potential Self: synonymous with the Universal Human, a full spectrum self, whose consciousness is stabilized and who has fully integrated all levels of selves: body, local self, personal essence, Essential Self and Universal Self within the quantum potential field, including great avatars and master teachers that most attract us.

References

Other books and DVDs by Barbara Marx Hubbard include:

Emergence: The Shift from Ego to Essence

Conscious Evolution: Awakening the Power of Our Social Potential

The Hunger of Eve: One Woman's Odyssey toward the Future

The Evolutionary Journey: Your Guide to a Positive Future

Revelation: Our Crisis is a Birth — An Evolutionary Interpretation of the New Testament

Evolutionary Communion (Guidebook and CD)

Humanity Ascending Documentary Series: (DVD)
· *Our Story*
· *Visions of a Universal Humanity*

All books, CDs and DVDs by Barbara Marx Hubbard can be purchased from her website:
www.barbaramarxhubbard.com

Related Works by Other Authors

The Mother of Invention: The Legacy of Barbara Marx Hubbard and the Future of You by Neale Donald Walsch

The Co-Creator's Handbook: An Experiential Guide for Discovering Your Life's Purpose and Building a Co-Creative Society by Carolyn Anderson with Katharine Roske